Tony Mitton

MEGA GREEK MYTH RAPS

Illustrated by Martin Chatterton

For Dad and Ruth
with love from Tony

ORCHARD BOOKS
96 Leonard Street, London, EC2A 4XD
Orchard Books Australia
Unit 31/56 O'Riordan Street, Alexandria, NSW 2015
First published in Great Britain in 2000
First paperback edition 2001
Text © Tony Mitton 2000
Illustrations © Martin Chatterton 2000
The rights of Tony Mitton to be identified as the author
and Martin Chatterton as the illustrator of this work
have been asserted by them in accordance with the
Copyright, Designs and Patents Act, 1988.
A CIP catalogue record for this book is available
from the British Library.
ISBN 1 84121 801 4 (hardback)
ISBN 1 84121 803 0 (paperback)
1 3 5 7 9 10 8 6 4 2 (hardback)
1 3 5 7 9 10 8 6 4 2 (paperback)
Printed in Great Britain

CONTENTS

Greedy Guy Rap

Well, now, folks,
have you had a look round?
Seen all the rubble
on the hot Greek ground?

A lot of it's crumbled
away into dust.
There's just an odd pillar
and a broken-up bust.
But they can remind us
that way back then,
a whole scene was happening
for gods and for men.

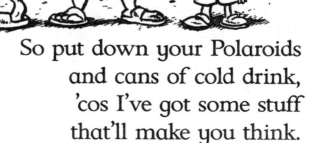

So put down your Polaroids
and cans of cold drink,
'cos I've got some stuff
that'll make you think.

I know some tales
from those old Greek times.
Just give me respect
and I'll rap 'em in rhymes.
Listen to me, yeah,
and hear me sing.
I'll start with a story
'bout a greedy Greek king.

His name was Midas.
He was crazy 'bout gold.
And he already had
a lotta money, I'm told.

Well, one day, early,
round about dawn,
he was taking a stroll
when he heard a yawn.
And, under a rose bush,
sprawled in a heap,
was a chubby old satyr,
waking from sleep.

(A satyr's a creature
half-goat and half-man.
Try to imagine
that if you can!)

7

The satyr was bleary
and smelling of wine,
but he stretched and smiled,
then he spoke real fine.

"Sorry, Daddy Midas,"
the satyr said,
"but I got real tired
and couldn't find a bed.
I was out with Dionysus,
the god of the grape.
We partied too much -
I was in bad shape.

I hope you don't mind
that I crashed in your garden.
So I'll just say, 'Thanks',
and, 'I beg your pardon'."

When Midas heard the satyr
was the pal of a god,
he gave him a smile
and a wink and a nod.
(In the days of the Greeks
the gods got respect.
You didn't mess with them
'cos you might get wrecked!)

Midas asked the satyr back
to get cleaned up.
Then he offered him wine
in a fine gold cup.

"Well," said the satyr,
as he took a deep sip,
"For a mortal kind of dude
you seem real hip.
You've poured me good wine
and put fruit in my dish,
so, just to say thanks,
I wanna shoot you a wish.

Tell me one thing
you'd like me to grant,
and I'll make it happen,
just see if I can't!"

King Midas turned over
what he'd just been told.
Then his eyes began to glitter
at the thought of...

"Beauty is neat
and power is cool.
But gold is the stuff
that makes me drool.

So I'm asking you, Satyr,
would it be too much
to grant me the power
of a golden touch?
To make it happen
that whatever I hold
or tickle or tap
turns into bright gold?"

12

The satyr went quiet.
He rolled round his eyes.
"Are you sure, King Midas?
Do you think that's wise?
It could get tricky,
if you know what I mean.
A golden touch…
that's a heavy scene.

Maybe you'd like
to try a different thing?
There ain't no hurry.
You can wish again, King."

Midas cracked back,
"Oh, is it too tough?
Maybe your magic
ain't solid enough?
But gold is the stuff
that I most want to see.
Are you catching my drift?
Please do it for me!"
The satyr said, "Midas,
I see that you're set.
I hope that you'll like
what you're going to get.

The wish was a way
that I tried to be nice.
Gold *looks* warm
but it's cold as ice."

So, saying goodbye,
by the light of the sun,
the satyr cut loose
with the gold wish done.

King Midas thought, "Hmm.
Have I been dim?
Maybe I ought to have
listened to him.
A wish like that
won't ever come true.
It can't be a thing
that a satyr can do.

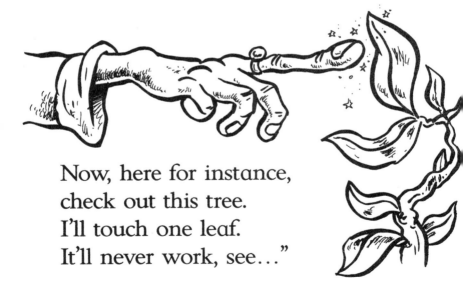

Now, here for instance,
check out this tree.
I'll touch one leaf.
It'll never work, see…"

He fingered the leaf.
It felt kind of cold.
And then it turned brittle
and bright like - GOLD!
Midas jumped high
hit a branch - slam-dunk!
The whole tree glistened -
leaves, boughs and trunk.

Midas started hopping
and leaping around,
leaving gold footprints
all over the ground.

"Wow!" whooped Midas.
"My wish has come true.
I'm gonna get gold.
Wa-hey and yahoo!"

He called all his servants
from greatest to least.
"Now go and get ready
one fabulous feast.
Bring everyone over
to see a surprise.
I'll do a live demo
in front of their eyes."

Well, all of his subjects
and his fancy friends came.
It sounded like Midas
had a real good game.
And while they all goggled,
King Midas made gold
from all kinds of things
that they gave him to hold.

Then, when he'd amazed them
with glittering skill,
he cried, "To the feast now!
Let's all eat our fill."

He lifted some cake
with a look of delight -
but his teeth nearly broke
when he took a big bite.

He grabbed for his goblet
to quench his deep thirst -
but the drink turned to gold
and he wailed and he cursed.
"When I got wishing,
I just didn't think
that my food would turn golden
and also my drink.

21

"I'll die of starvation.
What can I do?
I wish I was normal.
Oh, boo-hoo-hoo!"

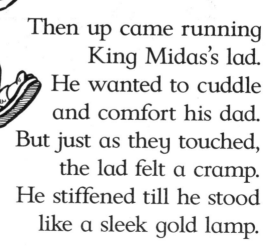

Then up came running
King Midas's lad.
He wanted to cuddle
and comfort his dad.
But just as they touched,
the lad felt a cramp.
He stiffened till he stood
like a sleek gold lamp.

"No!" cried Midas.
"That was my son!
What have I wished for?
What have I done?
I thought a golden touch
was bound to bring joy.
But it's cost me my life -
and I've lost my boy!

"That satyr was right
when he warned about gold.
It's hard and it's horrid
and ever so cold.
I wish I could ask him
to take off the spell,
turn my touch normal
and make my boy well."

"I'm glad to hear you say so,"
a voice said out loud.
And there stood the satyr
at the front of the crowd.

"Oh," said Midas,
down on his knees,
"Do it, dear Satyr,
do it now, please!
I've been so greedy.
I've been such a fool.
Gold's real cold,
but it sure ain't cool."

And, as Midas spoke
those words - well, hey! -
the gold kind of softened,
and vanished away.
His son gave a shiver.

Ooh, brrr! Dad, I'm chilly.
It feels like I froze
for a mo - but that's silly!

"Yo!" cried Midas.
"The gold spell is gone!
The nightmare is over,
so let's party on.
My cold golden touch
is over and done.
So now *that's* finished
we can really have fun!"

OK, folks,
my story's complete.
So jump in this boat,
'cos we're going to Crete.

Fly Guy Rap

Well, now, folks,
that wasn't too far.
A bit of a boat trip
and here we are!
The place may look
like a holiday resort.
But once it was ruled
by a real mean sort.

Bad old Minos
was that cruel King of Crete.
He lived in a palace
that couldn't be beat.

Minos

Daedalus

It was built by the best
designer he could find,
a guy from Greece
with a brilliant mind.
His name was Daedalus,
And, boy, was he clever!
He always said, "Maybe…"
and he never said, "Never".

He had a son, Icarus,
a slick young lad,
who didn't have brains
like his smart old dad.
He didn't like to puzzle
or to work things out.
All he did was doze
or dawdle about.

He'd rather lie around
with a fan on the beach,
fixing up his tan
or sucking on a peach.

Now, Minos's palace
was fancy and fine.
But it also had a clever,
yes, a cunning design.

To find your way around it
you had to have the plan.
And this belonged to Minos,
for he was The Man.
The palace held a maze
with a Minotaur inside,
and this was a monster
Minos needed to hide.

Daedalus had made the maze.
He had it in his head.
So Minos kept him prisoner
and this is what he said,

"You'll have to hang out here,
locked up in a tower.
It's no use to hassle,
'cos I've got The Power.
So don't try escaping,
and don't get hip.
This here's my kingdom.
I own every ship.

Besides, in your tower,
You'll be laid-back and free,
with many an hour
to invent things for me.
So send out for tools,
or for wood, string and glue.
Just think of the things
you can dream up to do!

Invent something handy,
and have a nice stay."
Then Minos slammed the door
as he locked them away.

"We're stuck here!" wailed Icarus,
beginning to cry.

The only way out
Would be if we could fly.

"Fly…wings…feathers…"
came Daedalus's words.
And he went to the window
to look at the birds.
He watched how they flapped,
how they floated and flew.
And he dreamed up a scheme
that was tricky to do.

He sprinkled some crumbs
so the seagulls could feed,
then he waited to gather
all the feathers he'd need.

And, feather by feather,
yes, day by day,
he carefully stashed
those feathers away.

And working by candlelight,
night after night,
he worked up some wings
they could use to take flight.

Wings held together
with wax dripped from candles,
and straps recycled
from old pairs of sandals.

One set for Daedalus,
another for Ic.
"Say!" said his son,
"What a neat, cool trick!"

"OK," said Daedalus,
"But listen to me.
Up there's the sun.
Down there's the sea.

Keep in-between them
and try not to fool.
Fly straight and steady.
The word is *cool.*

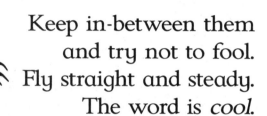

Fly too high
where the sun's real hot,
y'know what'll happen?
It'll melt the lot."

They put on their wings,
and they strapped them up tight.
"Get ready," said Ded,
"we're off on our flight."
They both took a breath.
They leapt from the sill…
and then they were flying -
wow! What a thrill!

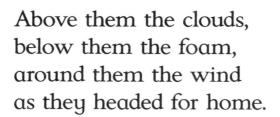

Above them the clouds,
below them the foam,
around them the wind
as they headed for home.

Minos's soldiers
got mad on the beach.
They shouted and shot,
but their arrows couldn't reach.
"Yah!" yelled Icarus.
"You're useless! You missed!"
Minos looked mean
and he shook his fist.

Icarus giggled
and let out a whoop,
then, just for the hell of it,
did a deep swoop.
"Wicked!" cried Icarus.

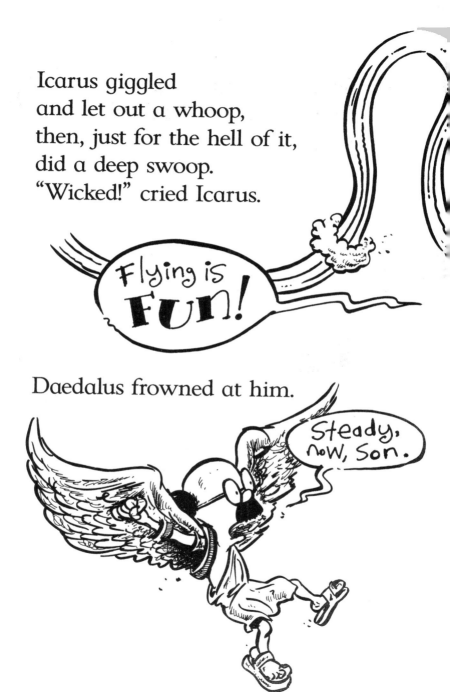

Daedalus frowned at him.

But Icarus was rapping,
"We're free, Dad, we're free!"
Then he did a neat loop
as he shrieked out, "Wheee!

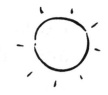

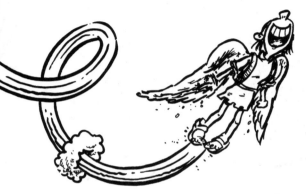

Now I've got wings
and I'm up in the air.
The sun's in my face
and the wind's in my hair.
I wonder how fast
and how high I can go?
Are you ready to rumble?
Get this. Yo!"

He took a deep gulp
and he seemed to change gear.
He threw back his head
and he showed no fear.
"The sky is my limit.
I'll try for a ton."
Then, flashing his feathers,
he flew for the sun.

His limbs didn't falter.
His face didn't flicker.
So soon he was soaring up
higher and quicker.

But, just as his dad warned,
the sun was like flame.
It loosened the feathers
and out they came.
He flapped and he fluttered.
He let out a cry.
His wings came to pieces
and he fell from the sky.

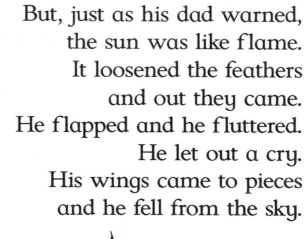

Daedalus saw it all,
but couldn't fly faster.
He couldn't do anything
to stop the disaster.
"Drat!" said Daedalus.
"I knew he'd make a hash."
Icarus said nothing but,

The story has to end here.
So, what do we find?
It doesn't always pay
to have a great mind.
But don't be like Icarus,
sticky and sad.
If you're going flying,
please listen to your dad!

47

RAP RHYMES
by Tony Mitton
Illustrated by Martin Chatterton

Collect all the books in this award-winning series!

Look out for these Greek Myth Raps!

Rap Rhymes are available from all good bookshops,
or can be ordered direct from the publisher:
Orchard Books, PO BOX 29, Douglas IM99 1BQ
Credit card orders please telephone 01624 836000
or fax 01624 837033
or e-mail: bookshop@enterprise.net for details.

To order please quote title, author and ISBN
and your full name and address.
Cheques and postal orders should be
made payable to 'Bookpost plc'.
Postage and packing is FREE within the UK
(overseas customers should add £1.00 per book).

Prices and availability are subject to change.